JOURNALING
THE BYWAYS OF
Lifetime
Journeys

AUDREY BROWN LIGHTBODY

WESTBOW
PRESS®
A DIVISION OF THOMAS NELSON
& ZONDERVAN

WestBow Press books may be ordered through booksellers or by contacting:

WestBow Press
A Division of Thomas Nelson & Zondervan
1663 Liberty Drive
Bloomington, IN 47403
www.westbowpress.com
1 (866) 928-1240

ISBN: 978-1-5127-9761-9 (sc)
ISBN: 978-1-5127-9762-6 (hc)
ISBN: 978-1-5127-9760-2 (e)

Library of Congress Control Number: 2017912005

Print information available on the last page.

WestBow Press rev. date: 08/16/2017

for my daughter, Joyce

Contents

The Midpoint of the Journey

The Ending of the Journey

Introduction

This is a book about journeying. The *Merriam-Webster* dictionary defines *journey* as:

> (1) Something suggesting travel or passage from one place to another: the journey from youth to maturity, a journey through time; (2) an act or instance of traveling from one place to another: Trip. A three day journey—going on a long journey.[1]

Based on this definition, you might assume that everyone is on a journey. In my earlier book, *Faith Is the Journey,* I began the introduction with words that also seem apropos for this book:

> As I began to think of journeys, I came to the realization that my vision was very limited. I tended to think of journeys as being those extended trips that take me to new locations, new countries, new vistas of sightseeing. I called a journey those trips that I took to foreign countries. I called a journey those movements I made to new homes from Massachusetts to Pennsylvania to California. I called it a journey when my experiences brought me to natural wonders— these were journeys.[2]

In your daily living, you might think of a journey as a trip to see family members who live at a distance, as a planned vacation, or as seeing the many wonders of the world. Most of us do not consider daily living as a journey.

Your life journey takes an entire lifetime, whether short or long. In the midst of that journey, there are other byways that connect, interact, and change your life journey. These have to do with a wide variety of life's moments. Some journeys are uniquely your own, but some—maybe even most—connect with other people's journeys, and, in turn, they may add to the journey, the way of journeying, and the changing of more than one journey. We might not have a plan that requires thinking about many byways; they just happen and so do the consequences of the byway. Some of these byways can be personal, and some go far afield because of our interest in a particular place or subject.

This book is in journal form. One cannot miss the connection of journal and journey, both referring to a day. Journals are made up of days, as are journeys. These journal entries are not daily writings but captured thoughts as one moves through life and discovers vital ideas that need to be a part of a lifetime journey.

In this book we will examine the journal of a woman named Lydia—not a real person but a woman who shares her journal days with every person who posts important happenings as they move through life. Lydia is, in fact, every woman who sees herself as a journeyer, sees her life as a lifetime journey, and sees that it also contains many byways and a variety of journeys.

I chose the name Lydia from the Bible (Acts 16:14). She was a businesswoman, a seller of purple cloth. You can assume that she made many journeys as she traveled, selling her royal purple wares. You can imagine that the biblical Lydia kept a journal of her trips and her sales and even of the people she met.

In *Journaling the Byways of Lifetime Journeys*, Lydia will share some of the places she visits—some vital, some not serious but all a part of the lifetime journey. Most of them could be a part of anyone's journey. There are many other byways that could be included, but in this journal, Lydia has selected the byways that are vital in her life. In walking through the journal, you may see journeying in new ways.

Journaling the Byways of Lifetime Journeys, told mostly in poetic form, is not really a journal about a specific person; rather, it is as if Lydia takes byways that may be a way to change and enlarge the understanding of a single person's journey. In addition to Lydia's journal entries in poetic form, Lydia has included "Thoughts for Reflection" in prose form. These thoughts have led to her daily penning of her journal.

As you wander through Lydia's byways and journals, may these words enrich your own life journey as you look at life through a different lens and find your own byways to fulfill God's plan.

A Journal Entry

What Makes Up a Journey?

There can be the starting point—the beginning,
> there can be anticipation—the rushing toward,
> there can be the planning—the humdrum tasks,
> there can be the sense of discovery—the very newness,
> there can be the fitting together,
>> even the building of the planned journey,
> there can be the wonder—the awesomeness,
> there can be joy unbounded,
> there can be the surprise—the unknowing.

There can be a middle point—
> there can be a time when one looks
>> at what has gone before and remembers,
>> looks ahead, and questions where the future leads,
> there can be the planning,
> there can be different tangents,
> there can be a change of direction—
>> a kind of newness, of discovery, even of wonder,
>> or perhaps a new commitment to what has gone before.

There can be the discovery of journeys within the life journey,
> there can be an ending point,
>> the time when one can let it go,
>> when there can be rejoicing over the journey,
> there can be the sense of gladness—"it is finished."
> there can be a sense of sadness—the grief of loss,
> there can be the closing point—the ending.

All of this makes up the journey, any journey, all journeys—
> can these thoughts be a parallel for life journeying?
How will I do my journeying?

The Beginning of the Journey

Thoughts for Reflection

The Lifetime Journey Begins with the Journey into Self

The journal begins with the lifetime journey and must begin with the self.

There must be a beginning point. That would be within a mother's womb as the fetus produced by two people who may or may not have decided about starting a new life journey. They may or may not have had a plan. These two people may have studied what this would mean in their lives. Cost may be a factor in creating a family. Unlike a trip, this journey will have been done without the participation of the fetus. This is your unique beginning point, the start of the lifetime journey—new life on a new journey.

The "unplanning" of the lifetime journey continues. It is developed in the early years by others, fitting into some basic terms. Psychologist and psychoanalyst Erik Erikson named eight basic stages of life and associated each with a specific psychosocial development. These eight stages, spanning from birth to death, are split into general age ranges:

1. infant (hope)
2. toddler (will)
3. preschooler (purpose)
4. school-age child (competence)
5. adolescent (fidelity)
6. young adult (love)
7. middle-aged adult (care)
8. older adult (wisdom)

These stages of life form stops along the way, and they must be a part of your itinerary. But you may discover something larger on the journey forward.

After the beginning, you move into the byways—the increasing sense of self as a person. These are not seen as anything other than your natural growth, but they do make a difference in a person and, by extension, in society. These pathways seem to encompass the early years and take you to middle age.

Lydia (every woman) has chosen five areas that seem to have a dynamic impact on her sense of self, starting at the beginning point and moving toward the midpoint. There are many other byways in these early years, but those journaled in this part of the journey include family, the senses, words, music, and the emotions.

Walk with Lydia as she emerges into a self.

A Journal Entry

Beginning the Lifetime Journey

The Self

The journey began without my knowledge.
It began in a dream between two people,
      two creative urges, and
      it became a journey into self.
That early dream tattooed itself
      into my very being.
I was created, and now I am creating,
      creating a self.
It is now my journey into a self.
This journey into self will span ages, ideas—
      intermingling,
      interconnecting,
      and companionship.
This journey into self will also demand
      solitude,
      solitariness,
      and quiet times with just the self.
My journey into self, in its beginning,
      was without plan,
      very much on instinct,
      very much as learner,
      absorbing little bits
            of knowledge, emotions,
            of pitfalls, of just being.
My journey continues on and on—
      the dailiness, the seeking,
      the joys, the sorrows,
      the surprises, the failures,

the growth, the pulsing beat of life.
All these continually change my journey and
cause the self to be determined.
The journey into self, like its beginning,
cannot be planned far ahead and
will not have a known ending
because the journey into self is
the plan of God.

Thoughts for Reflection

The Journey into Family

Family is an enormous subject. There is the immediate family into which you are born, or there may be an adopted family. There is the extended family of aunts, uncles, grandparents, nieces, nephews, cousins, and in-laws. There are also people with whom there is such a close relationship that they are included as family. There are those who may have come from other lands and make up your ancestry. Then, of course, there is the human family—all people.

Looking into families, there are many kinds. Certain geographic groups may be classified as family, as may foods, diseases, and medicine. There are geographic families and racially diverse family groups. There are religious family groupings. There are even subsets within these groupings. You can move from family into other factions: communities, states, countries, and continents. Thus, you understand the whole world of human families is a part of the family of earth and, most fully, the family of God.

Early in the journey of finding the self is the realization that the intersection of your life with the nuclear family makes differences in the lives of others and adds to the sense of self. The family values will add or detract as you move along the pathway to discovering your unique self.

As you look at the variety of families in the world, it becomes obvious that one little self can reach out and grab much more of life than what at first might seem possible. In so doing, the individual makes changes in the self. The world can also reach out with such a variety of influences that the self can never be the same again.

Family plays an important role in the whole life journey. Family and its meaning may change with age, with world events, and with the finding of new paths. But family must speak, not only at the beginning point but at the midpoint and ending point as well.

A Journal Entry

A Family Journey

Creating God, look on us,
        children of God, child in family,
        children of creation,
        creating children within the universe.
God, we find ourselves creatures
        within the world of family,
        within your creating power,
        within the universe
                of journeyers that we would create
                of diversity, of individuality,
                and finally, still as children of God.
Invisible threads, weaving in and out, around,
        ephemeral but touching each person.
Invisible threads, binding, binding
        in ways unknown,
        in time lapses,
        in fragments of thought,
        in spiritual ties to one another.
Invisible threads, bound into family,
        freed into artistic creativity,
        freed to make the journey
        to finding one's self in family,
        to one another and into created world.
        to finding oneself and all in the family.
Creating God, guide us in family to journey's end.

The Daughter/Sister Journey

This journey began before my knowledge,
     tattooed itself into my very being.
The journey began with a night of love,
of watery warmth in a human bowl,
the stress, the pain, the work of delivery
and then the entry into the loving warmth
     of human arms.
I know other persons: mother, father, siblings.
I became one of others
     to become a binding force to make family,
     and thus started on the journey to creating family.
What did it mean to be a daughter/sister in family,
     lessons that would change as the years progressed
     but always a part of the journey,
          learning how to be a part of the whole,
          learning how to be uniquely myself,
          learning how to be a creative person?
As I grew older, I saw myself as an artist;
     I needed to stand alone,
     sorting out color, form, dimension,
     and the interplay within myself and in the world about me,
     learning, always learning lessons of relationship in art and
     family.
The journey continues toward God's eternity.

The Mother Journey[3]

She was not always a mother—she had her own journey;
>out of her journey, she grew and became the person
who bore the children, trained the children,
>loved all her children.
As a mother, she was a dynamo as well as the dispenser of
>little bits of wisdom,
>little drops of goodness,
>little moments of joyous loving.
It was in the little things she exemplified that
>I learned of life,
>I found beauty; I met God.
Oh, it was not that Mother did not
>do the big things:
>care for family unendingly,
>lead and prod and guide
>and contribute her helpfulness to the world.
Rather, it was in the
>mostly unthought-through acts,
>the passing generosities of spirit,
>the sterling silverness of a
>commitment to be the best.
I see her, standing tall, this mother-woman
>who showed the family
>the value of all life,
>who guided my journey into
>>a maturity of which I am not ashamed.
Like building blocks, I saw
>little moments create new understanding,
>new pathways whereon to walk,
>life-giving force for our tomorrows.
The journey continues toward God's eternity.

The Son/Brother Journey[4]

This journey began before his knowledge,
      tattooed itself into his very being.
The journey began with a night of love,
of watery warmth in a human bowl,
the stress, the pain, the work of delivery
and then the entry into the loving warmth
      of human arms.
He knew other persons: mother, father, siblings;
he became one of others
to become a binding force to make family
and, thus, started his part on the journey to creating family.
The child stood amid others: a son, a brother, in family,
    learning how to be a part of the whole,
    learning how to be uniquely himself,
    learning how to be a creative person,
    learning how to fit into family mode.
He knew the journey into words
      were to be his nemesis;
      as a child he was great with rote learning,
      but abstract ideas were more difficult;
          this family of his were all people
          to whom ideas were common coinage,
     so he learned from family
         how to be like them,
         how to share his joy, his friendship,
         how to share his relationship individually
            with each of us in family,
            and grow into his self.
The journey continues toward God's eternity.

The Father Journey

He was not always a father—he had his own journey;
     out of his journey, he grew and became the person
     who furnished the seed for family,
     who guided the children,
     who labored to provide food,
     who was the "man" figure.
As a father, his life was just ordinary,
     caught up in work, his faith, his family,
     daily giving lessons that life demands
          attention,
          that tasks help us grow,
          that love binds a family together.
He made beauty in his carpentering
     as he finished and refinished items
          for our home,
          for our church,
          for each of us, individually.
Gardening was his love, and he made it lovely—
     so that we enjoyed vegetables
          fresh from the garden,
          flowers planted and cared for lovingly,
     teaching us ways to make beauty,
          to enjoy the richness
          of what the earth provided.
Teaching us lessons for living—
     to be responsible,
     to help others, as he did regularly,
     to work hard and earn your living,
     to know that a loving father
          speaks of God's continuing love.
The journey continues in God's family until journey's end.

Thoughts for Reflection

A Byway on the Journey into Self—the Senses

Sometimes a trip will have the side stops to places you have been before, but you decide that you will go there anyway and look for newness and a greater understanding of this place, this scene. Such a place in the life journey is the need to take a look at the senses.

Most people have come equipped with all the body parts that allow humans to see, hear, smell, touch, and speak. The beginning part of the journey is how you learn to use these organs that will be with you, hopefully, through all of a lifetime. As you journey, as you age, you need to make greater use of them and learn more, not just simply gain the basic knowledge. The need to expand it, to bring newness into your life, and to make full use of all of your faculties is a continuing part of the byway into the senses. This journey changes with age and with the development into a full adult human being.

Beyond the five senses, other senses must be developed because there is no external body part to make its function obvious. There are no tattooed parts that come from the unplanned beginning. There is a sense that explains the perception of your body in relation to gravity, movement, and balance. This sense measures acceleration, g-force, body movements, and head position. There is a sense that allows you to know the relative position of neighboring parts of the body and the strength of effort employed in movement. This sense is very important, as it lets you know exactly where the body parts are and how to plan your movements.

How amazing it is to understand that all these senses can function together and separately as well and make a self that will grow into the person on a lifetime journey.

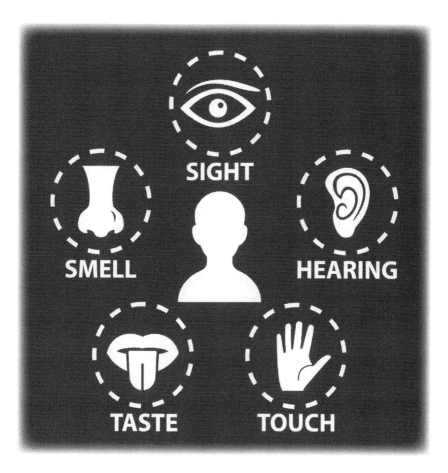

A Journal Entry

Journey into the Senses

This place of visitation began
     without my knowledge,
     tattooed itself into my very being.
I came equipped with ears and eyes,
     nose and mouth,
     tactile sense and querying mind.
There it was: the reason for me to begin
     my rediscovery journey into my senses.

Here I am, this creature with the inborn faculties
     that I must begin to explore
     as I make my way on the journey of life.
I must be awake to the possibility
     that even in my earliest days,
     without planning, without being aware
       of the wonders that are to come,
     I am on a journey of discovery—
of finding whatever happens
       in creative knowledge
       that God is in my senses.

I have been blessed with *eyes* that reflect beauty—
     that I can use my eyes for seeing,
     to learn as I grow
     into how to focus, how to open and close,
     how to let light into my being,
     how to read,
     how to speak through my eyes,
     how to measure space,
     how to know immensities

beyond my littleness—
that out there God holds the power.

I have been so blessed with a *nose* to
differentiate the various aromas
that assail me day by day,
to be able to smell the roses,
to be able to draw in the sea air,
to be able to wrinkle my nose
at the bad smells
to enjoy the deliciousness of
God's creation.

I have been blessed with *ears* that can
hear the myriad sounds of daily life,
that also become attuned to
the tiny whispers that lead to newness,
and the raucous shouts that tell
of a teeming world fraught
with good and evil,
with opportunities to hear
the sonorous songs of the ages,
and the hip-hop tunes that speak of now.
with times of uplifting marches
to a distant drummer,
and the caustic pronouncements
of insanity in a world gone mad,
with words of love in the world of
God's creative power.
I have been blessed with a *mouth* that can
communicate with words,
share kisses of love,
speak in great orations,
or whisper special secrets;
that can utter words of cursing

or of blessing,
that can tell a child of love,
of courage, of joy,
and change a life and
maybe, even a world;
that leads into the mystery of
God's will.

I have been blessed with a sense of *touch,*
of feeling, of throbbing life,
of actual pain,
of being able to hold within myself
so much joy, deep happiness,
so much anguish, sorrow,
the texture of friendship,
the strength of well-trained muscles,
the clasping of hands with others,
in clapping and in prayer, and
in throwing upraised hands in exuberance,
in knowing fingertips on glory
and the figurative touching of the hand of God.

I need to be aware that all of these senses
as I first knew them;
know that like any journey,
I will need to give constant attention and care,
know that growing and aging and illness
will take their toll and never be the same;
that I will continue my voyage of discovery
and find changes in myself,
and in the world around me,
and in my understanding
of my life journey.
This different creation as I journey
into the senses will
teach me to trust the plan of God.

Thoughts for Reflection

Another Byway into the Journey to Self—the Landscape of Words

Numerous books and articles have been written about the beginning of language. They suggest that millions of years or, even more recently, fifty thousand years ago language communication began. Biblical stories suggest that when God created man and woman, he talked with them in the Garden of Eden. It is interesting to note that from the very beginning, God must have created a thinking person. There are all kinds of theories about the beginning of language and what caused it, but clearly there is no real beginning knowledge.

So many questions have been asked through the ages that attempt to explain language, spoken or written. Spoken words would have come first, but how were they created. How did spoken words come about? Was sign language the very beginning of words? Is the ability for language built into your genomes? Even an infant reacts to cooing, loving sounds. Children know when they have displeased an adult from the tone of the spoken words. There are so many questions about words and speaking and first knowledge.

Written words followed, but what instinct was there that caused someone to put words into tangible form. In early pictographs, you see a form of writing—pictures telling a story. The need for written language had to have been caused by some immediate need to keep control of trade or ownership. Drawings became symbols that could be used to show what belonged to a person.

The questions keep tumbling upon themselves. When were the words spelled out? What implements were used? What about other languages in both spoken and written form? How were people able to interpret those languages into common verbiage for outsiders?

When thinking of your "self," at what point do you become aware of words, other than just as sounds? Even using good words, what are the possibilities for misunderstanding the meaning and intent, behind "words".

You can try to imagine a world without words; you can try to visualize how you could function in a world without words—it cannot be done. Words are a vital step on the journey to self.

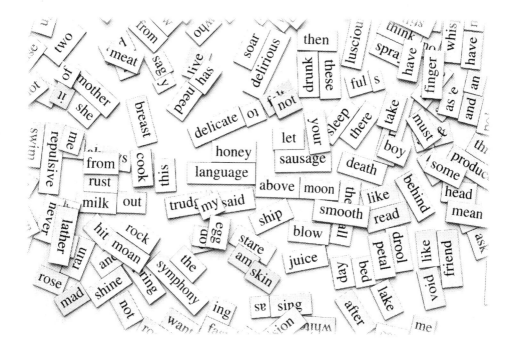

A Journal Entry

Journey into Words

This journey began without my knowledge,
　　　tattooed itself into my very being.
I came equipped with the ability
　　　to find words, to make sentences,
　　　to put words on paper,
　　　to make changes in life.
There it was: the reason for me to begin
　　　my journey into my words.

Into the life journey comes one important part—
something about which we think little,
　　　　at the beginning point we do not do
　　　　　　any real planning by ourselves.
　　　　We do not think about that trip, without which
　　　　　　much of the rest of our journeys
　　　　　　would not occur;
　　　　that is the journey into *words*;
　　　　　　words can be heard, seen, spoken,
　　　　　　touched, written,
　　　　　　offer even a sense of smell.
　　　Words are the coinage of our lives.
Even as one or more senses are taken away,
　　　　　　we can still know words in some form.
　　　Words are filled with different meanings,
　　words can be different parts of speech,
　　words have the ability to hurt or bless
　　　　　or change our moods,
　　　　　or even be reflective.
Words make up our language—very little in our being
　　　has more influence in our daily lives.

Words are omnipresent.
    Words can engender high moments in life,
    words can describe what we feel
        in awe and wonder;
        they can debase us or others.
    Words are everywhere—they make up
        the conversations of our lives,
        communications with others,
        even communication within ourselves.
    what kinds of words surround us?
Words make up the lingua franca of our countries:
    there can be many languages,
    many dialects,
    many unknown words—
    words whose meanings are alien to us,
    much to ponder as we listen,
        as we see words alone
        and in sentences;
        and yet there is a difference.
        Some words are nouns
        and some have become verbs—
            if not the same, but similar.
        Some words are passive and some have the potential
            for being active.
    By adding "ing" to a word can make words transformative;
        have the power of changing my world.
        some words are simply statements,
            others seem more personal.
There are words that have
        been made into games,
there are words that fall into clusters,
        words that change with the addition of certain letters
            that really give new meaning.
The trip into words can offer
    a potpourri of challenging thoughts,

the opportunity to be a communicator,
the time to hear and speak God's word—
     in ways unknown, in time lapses,
     in fragments of thought,
     in spiritual ties that lead into deeper meaning
          in my conversing with the God of all.

Thoughts for Reflection

Another Byway into the Journey to Self—the Landscape of Music

Where did music come from? Is it something that people, long ago, discovered, or did people invent it? Humans discovered what is primal in nature—the music of the spheres within the world. There is recognition of the sounds that are emitted through animals, basic to humans, even in the air about all nature. There is the origin of music from naturally occurring sounds and rhythms. Music was within humans, probably prior to recorded history. Is music something that is a part of the universe, or have humans made it a creation of their minds?

Music is a force that is capable of doing many things, both within a person and within a whole world. Music is in your very bone marrow and within your whole being. Humans react differently to music, somewhat based upon the person's culture and one's own intrinsic being. Music lifts your thoughts above the ordinariness of every day.

There is such a variety of kinds of music. There are very simple one-note music sounds and the complexity of the great compositions. There are differences in tone, timbre, tempo, and pitch. There are differences in how you react to music, based on culture, location, and circumstances.

Music has brought about the creation of instruments in such a wide variety that you could hardly list them. Humans have created this variety to plumb the heights and depths of making music soar in unexplainable wonder within the human soul.

The creation of music called for scales and words and infinitesimal notations in order to make music live through many generations. There is wonder that humans can feel the music within their selves in such a way that people anywhere may be uplifted or may feel joy, sadness, and an unknown urging to make life more beautiful. Music has its own terminology.

These words from John Denver say it so well:

"Music does bring people together. It allows us to experience the same emotions. People everywhere are the same in heart and spirit. No matter what language we speak, what color we are, the form of our politics or the expression of our love and our faith, music proves: We are the same."[5]

A Journal Entry

Journey into Music

This journey began without my knowledge,
      tattooed itself into my very being.
I came equipped with the ability
      to hear the music, to join the song,
      to feel the beat, to understand
         the feelings welling up inside me,
      to be at one within myself.
I first heard the music in a baby's lullaby—
      it calmed me, told me of care.
      I was safe, enfolded into harmony and love.
I grew to understand there was so much more—
I learned that music holds a whole container
      of feelings, of a beat,
      of rhythm that pervades all of nature,
      of cadence and deep undertones,
      of sonorous notes that lift my spirits,
      of dirge-like songs that hold
         all the sadness of the universe.
Music calls for instruments to emphasize variety—
      there is the beating of the human heart,
      there is the human voice speaking in different ways—
         whistling, clicking, coughing, yawning,
         cooing, singing, humming, clapping.
      There are too many instruments to name, but
      each flute or harp or trumpet speaks its own language,
      each drum or piano or carillon creates its own sonority.
People everywhere use music to celebrate
      the everydayness and the special occasions—
         social gatherings, sports events,
         recitals, symphony offerings,

marching off to war and parades,
weddings, christenings, funerals.
Music may be different all over the world—
it may reflect the culture, or a time period.
It may be folk music, traditional to one place,
Western, Eastern, from the far reaches of the earth,
classical, rock and roll, tonal or atonal,
it may be indigenous, baroque, religious,
but how it makes us feel is universal.
The importance of music—other than just enjoyment—can be felt
in reducing stress, physiologically, therapeutically,
assisting in movement, exercise, during surgery, dentistry,
alleviating pain for many medicinal purposes,
in brain development, emotional uplift,
and just enjoyment of the time spent listening,
making our lives more whole.
Music is one of the greatest creations of humans—
it expresses feelings in a person in ways that words cannot,
holds within its compositions the power to
draw millions from around the world into
breaking down barriers of hatred and evil,
of racism, sectionalism, different religions,
to find within its music: love, peace, passion, creativity,
to enchant the hearts of all people,
leading them into the heart of God.
God is in the music; God is the music.
My soul sings in praise for the music everywhere in God's realm.

Thoughts for Reflection

Another Byway into the Journey of Self—the Emotions

Here is another trip into familiar territory but an even greater need to look for new pathways as you cruise into emotions. The dictionary tells us that emotions are "an affective state of consciousness in which joy, sorrow, fear, hate, or the like is experienced, as distinguished from cognitive and volitional states of consciousness; any of the feelings of joy, sorrow, fear, hate, love, etc.; any strong agitation of the feelings actuated by experiencing love, hate, fear, etc., and usually accompanied by certain physiological changes, as increased heartbeat or respiration, and often overt manifestation, as crying or shaking"[6] (Dictionary.com).

Basic emotions allow you to regulate yourself in response to what is happening in the environment and opportunities found within and without. While there is no definitive list of basic emotions, one popular one contains six: fear, anger, sadness, disgust, surprise, and joy. These six have been found in every culture worldwide and even across cultures. This suggests that these are personal responses, individually, rather than ideas that grow out of the culture of a group.

The sense that we call extrasensory perception (ESP) means we get information not through our physical senses but from our own minds and inner feelings. ESP is also casually referred to as a sixth sense, gut instinct or hunch but is also felt as intuition. ESP contains several abilities: empathy, telepathy clairvoyance, and probably others that you inherit within yourself.

As you consider emotions, look at feelings. What are the differences between feelings and emotions? Emotions are a physical response to change, and feelings are the mental reactions to an emotion. Emotions actually precede feelings. Emotions can change easily from fear to security, or from being unfriendly to, perhaps, love;

this shows that emotions can be easily changeable, but the feelings you have may stay with you or grow over a lifetime. Emotions are physical; they can be measured objectively by a variety of means: blood flow, brain activity, facial expressions, and body stance. There is no such measuring of feelings, except in a larger sense—within the person. Emotions are something you can count on and easily understand, while feelings are often related to one particular person and seem confusing. Feelings reflect your personal associations; feelings are sparked by emotions and flamed into being because of the thoughts and images that you associate with a particular emotion.

Whereas emotions are one of those traits tattooed into a person from birth and a common factor to all, the meanings someone acquires *and* the feelings each person knows within the self are very personal. Feelings are or can be a part of your unique temperament and lived-out lifestyle. Feelings vary from person to person and from where a person lives to what is happening within your sphere of life. There can be many emotions that lead to various feelings. There can be many feelings connected to a particular emotion. A well-rounded person has both emotions and feelings.

A Journal Entry

Journey into the Emotions

This journey began without my knowledge,
     tattooed itself into my very being.
I came equipped with the ability
     to be aware of other feelings
          deep in my inmost being—
          not palpable, but real.
There it was: the reason for me to begin
     my landfall trip into my emotions.

Emotions are not senses;
     they change, often within minutes,
     they can make us into different persons,
     they are responses to situations—
          to people, both friends and foes,
          to physical difficulties,
          to the unknown,
          to pleasure and to grief,
          companions in our lives,
          come and go, changing.
Emotions are the hidden/open parts of ourselves.

There are so many kinds of emotions;
     some basic ones—
          anger, disgust, fear,
          happiness, sadness, surprise,
          and, of course, love.
     Out of these come other emotions
          that further define some of these emotions
          that have physical effects, and deep feelings
          that can change a person,

make one seem more human,
make one seem unattractive,
help us respond to our environment.
Emotions are important to human development.
I need to better understand this behavior
as I understand the feelings
that arise from emotions,
that I begin to make sense about my world
and know that in the deepest feeling,
God is there.
Therefore, I go willingly to this journey again.

A Journal Entry

Journey into Feelings

What are feelings? What do I mean when I talk about feelings?
> There are the feelings that are a part of touch,
> of illness, soreness, pain,
> of being mixed up, out of control,
> of the need to be alone, apart.

How do I identify the kinds of feelings?
> In my body, in my mind, in a gut instinct,
> from outside sources, from dreams,
> from people—both friends and foes—
> from God messages?

When do I need to acknowledge what causes these feelings
> that arise out of my emotions,
> out of my personal fantasies,
> out of relationships, out of family,
> out of emotional triggers,
> out of the little inner voice
>> that causes me, intuitively,
>>> to make better choices or
>>> to be aware of how I am seen and known?

> Where will feelings lead me on my journey
> to know my body better,
> to ponder my thoughts more deeply,
> to be creative in my planning,
> to take action in working for a better world,
> to make my senses, emotions, and feelings
> into a fitting place for God to reign,
> to seek wholeness and to find
> in this byway room for growth,
> to find peace within the plan of God?

35

The Midpoint of the Journey

Thoughts for Reflection

The Journal of the Journey's Midpoint

Journeys have a midpoint that occurs as people expand their horizons, both into the outer world and into a deeper sense of self with more depth and seeking greater understanding of their positions in the world.

The midpoint means continuing the journey of self, with its unremitting development of routine, of life with a lot of sameness, but it also causes you to reach out in new ways, inwardly. The midpoint forces you to not only continue the inner journey, but to reach out in ever-widening circles to that which includes the outward. Influences cause you to move from the solitary journey into one that realizes that there are a vast panoply of other resources that must become part of the journaling of the byways into lifetime journeys.

In the course of a lifetime, each person goes through numerous life-changing moments. These may be subsumed under major categories: body, mind, spirit, outside events, careers, families, and a general category that may seem unidentifiable. These may be unique to one individual or may affect much of the population, even in a global sense. As you consider some of these events, change will occur. As you act on where the journey leads, a change to the self may become obvious to others as well.

The action will move from the individual to the outside, global events. You can look at what is happening in the outer world and learn from these events about ways of coping with change. In this section inner self-reflections will become the first step into a new byway.

In the midpoint, Lydia will move on the byways of
family, routine, solitude, and change, and
the outer world—friendship, work, play, prayer, and
forms of government.

A Journal Entry

The Family Journey at Midpoint

Midpoint brings a sense of change in the area of family.
  We are fewer and yet more.
Here I stand at midpoint, older now,
  living a different life.
I am now an artist, mature now,
   I stand apart from family—my birth family—
     and yet bound by ties that could not be broken,
   still known as daughter/sister,
   still absorbing from the environment
     all that could be seen of dimension, form, and color,
   ready to add to my unique life palette,
   ready to seek to be more
     within an extended family.
I recognize many consistencies and
  even more inconsistencies.
I recognize that at midpoint the journey continues
  with routine, struggle, and a sense of
  leading toward God's eternity.

The son/brother a mature adult now—
   stands apart from family—and yet bound
    by ties that could not be broken
    as he assumed the man role—
     a worker at daily toil,
     and in his deeper moments,
     a writer of inspired verse
      to the world, to people, to God.
   Ready to create his own life journey
    in words and wondrous thoughts,

Ready to create a unique vision
for his life and for others.
The journey continues in God's family until life's end.

A second journey into family comes at midpoint—my new family:
a husband and children and the many ways
in which I find the journey changes:
I am the mother and the caregiver,
I am the dispenser of the little things—big ones too.
I must work in collaboration with the other new journeys.
My work, family activities and learning the lessons of integration
of so many others seeking to find their own unique journeys.
The journeys become pathways that lead into God's continuing love.

A Journal Entry

Journey into the Routine of Dailiness

It is midpoint in the life journey—
>   a time of life designated from
>   forty until …?
>   A time of becoming rooted,
>   a time to end some of the searching,
>   a time to become settled; a time to look farther ahead,
>   a time to enjoy where the journey leads.
In these midpoint years, there is the determining of a routine—
>   a time of knowing what happens on given days,
>   a calendaring of events and social responsibilities,
>   a need to be more deeply involved in family pursuits,
>   perhaps a time for sending forth sons and daughters,
>   no longer children, but young adults,
>   a time of looking at the daily tasks, over and over again,
>   of finding in the routine a happiness in the known, or
>   a time of being in the doldrums of so much sameness.
There is time for work, time for rest,
>   time for meals, time with family, time with friends.
The need to make time to be creative, time to find oneself
>   amid the regular schedule of dailiness,
>   amid the conflict of demands,
>   amid one's own need to break away from routine.
The midpoint years have the potential to
>   reinforce the sense that we are smothered by routine
>   and the future looks at a bleak sameness or
has the potential to draw one into newness,
has the potential to believe that God's plan for a life,
>   has both routine and challenge, and that there
>   is a purpose for the dailiness.

A Journal Entry

Journey into Solitude

Solitude is not something only for the midpoint—
      solitude was from the very beginning,
      solitude can create a world,
      something experienced without knowing its value,
      something that happened was in our genes.
Solitude carries with it silence, solitariness, and creativity—
      in the silence can be found the quiet thoughts,
      in the silence, in the solitude, I can listen.
      I can hear the inner voices calling me
            to new endeavors, deepening insights,
            to look into my very soul,
            to be—just to be.
Solitude almost demands solitariness—being alone
      with one's thoughts, with one's own person,
      forgetting the world, the daily concerns,
      listening for the still small voice
            that only comes when there is silence, solitariness,
            solitude,
      being at one with oneself and God,
      learning to be—just to be.
Out of solitude may come creativity—a new ability
      to find answers in an unanswerable world,
      to learn a way to new discoveries,
      to find new depths in one's soul-searching,
      to need to move from solitude into ways
            that reach out to others, to be at one with others,
            to create a new world that needs God's plan,
            to find in the busy world what solitude has shared
            and to be—just to be.

Out of the solitude, out of the silence, out of the solitariness,
out of the learning to be—just be—comes the need for something more:
    to put into action the thoughts, the need for others,
    to believe in God's plan and work unceasingly to attain the
    goal.

Thoughts for Reflection

Journey into Change at the Midpoint

Change is a word with two quite different meanings. There is money as change—coins received in place of bills or as payment when we receive money back. Loose change in the pockets may lead to finding an exciting way to use that money.

Change can also mean replacing one item with another. This happens when deciding to wear a different outfit or when you make a decision on the way to do work and then come up with another way to do it, changing your mind. All of life permits daring and excitement as you make other choices.

Change means that something has become different. Almost all of life is subject to change. Very few parts of life, society, or culture will not undergo change.

Change can be either a noun or a verb, meaning much the same in either case.

Change happens with varying effects on life in the here and now. There is a whole universe that speaks of how change made the world into what we see and understand about life. When there is little change, we find a society without much growth, content to stay bound in tedium. Yet there is a degree of happiness and pleasant living when serenity abounds.

In this midpoint time, looking at the effects on the various life journeys may lead to newness and transformation. This could be a welcome moment as you change byways, looking for something that will cause an interruption. With half of your life already past, it becomes time to see where this latter half will find guidance for the journey.

A Journal Entry

Changing Journeys

Change becomes another word to be scrutinized.
It is important to recognize the difference in our lives
      as we go through the journey,
        to recall the times that caused life to change in significant ways,
        to feel again those times in our lives
            that were life-changing moments, defining moments—
            those moments that mean we can never be the same
            again,
            those times when our lives go on a different course;
            these moments differ from individual to individual—
            some may seem insignificant, some radical
                a new way to be—just be.
Out of the dailiness, out of the solitude—
        how do I determine when those really important changes
        will cause me to become a different person?
How boring it would all be if change was not a part
        of the universe,
        of our individual lives,
        of the natural world we know,
        of space and heavenly bodies,
        of the global villages around the world.
If change is necessary in so many ways, how do we recognize
        the effects that devastating natural disasters
            will have on an individual?
            Who will be a part of an earthquake
                or hear of one in another part of the globe?
        Will this necessitate physical disruption
        that causes moving to another location,
        that changes how the family needs
            to reassess their living arrangements,

to strengthen the bonds of love and caring,
to decide on an individual basis how to adjust?
How do we recognize the effects of political disasters-—that show
little caring for
the poor, the homeless, the stranger,
the person striving to see people as being in God's image,
all persons being of worth and valued.
How do we recognize the effects of personal disasters—-
those that come about because
of illness, long times of being confined,
of mental stress, loss of cognitive response,
of job loss, financial capability loss,
of friends, of moving away,
loss of personal worth?
Disasters are major change agents, yet they have the ability
to cause us to change the journey, any kind of journey.

Change is caused by the events that happen within everyday living:
not disasters, but events that occur over and over again—
Change, like money that is returned in coinage, may just mean
that I have really only traded one formation in my life
for another one—having no significant difference in the way
I live.
Is there change that leads to multiple changes that may only be
temporary----
for given moments—or for a whole lifetime:
schooling, diet, medical emergencies, family functions,
social events, exercise, hobbies, rules, and just fun?
At the midpoint adding "*ing*" to the word means that making change
allows me to go to the mountaintop or to the valley of despair
as I perceive where change will lead me,
and decide on how to move ahead at the midpoint.
Will I perceive the hand of God in any kind of change and
learn to put my hand into God's welcoming hand of
love?

Thoughts for Reflection

Journaling the Journey into the Outer World

Looking at the outer world at the midpoint seems to have missed something in all the growing up years that lead into adulthood. Certainly we have contact with so many byways of the world outside of self and family and home. Tiny footsteps all along the lifetime journey have happened as friendships are formed, as teachers and knowledge lead to the understanding that there is a whole world into which we go. There are, at the midpoint, the matter of work and career, the changing face of play, and matters of faith. Learning of cities, states, country, and an entire world enlarge the growing vision as we move from infant (*hope*) to toddler (*will*) to preschooler (*purpose*) to school-age child (*competence*) to adolescent (*fidelity*) to young adult (*love*) to middle-aged adult (*care*). The psychosocial development has changed the self, even as life has come to the midpoint. Now the multiplicity of the other calls us to search in so many other byways that are more than the self.

The vision has been stretched, and now at the midpoint the journal must put down some new entry truths as the journeyer learns to see his or her self as one who shares what these new insights will reveal. Now, at the midpoint, the byway is not to the senses but, in a similar way, finding ourselves in the outside world, looking at the outer world and seeing within it the pathway forward to the ending point of the lifetime journey.

A Journal Entry

Journey into Friendship

I am moving forward into a universe
      that is more complex, more filled with the unknown,
      that causes me to take tiny steps into a wider world—
          a place where fearsome realities may await,
          where finding new insights may broaden my horizons,
          where I may experience joy unbounded or devastating
            loss,
              severe enough to change me deep inside.
With trembling, I set out on the journey to enlarge my circle,
      to enter into a relationship that goes beyond family,
      to dare to reach out to the different,
      to learn of other ways to see the world;
      to, perhaps, become a changeling as together we move,
          my friend and I, from the known, secure, regular life
          into exciting byways that challenge our very beings.
Friendship is a gift we offer to one another,
      a gift we receive from another person or persons.
Friendship happens from our early years, from so many sources—
      from the neighbor child who plays with abandon,
      from the school chum, who shares assignments,
      from summer camps and summer trips,
      from all the places that link ideas and concerns,
      from ties that bind us to one another.
Friends offer to us a gift of unadulterated love,
      that can survive movement away from each other,
      that can speak to us of sympathy, understanding, and closeness,
      that can build a world through written notes,
          or e-mail, or phone calls,
          or an unexplained visit that assures us

that friendship exists to let us know
that we are dear and ready to be tied together.
The gift of friendship has blessed my growing-up years
and now is such a treasure in the midpoint years:
in all the tragedies and joys and seeming "lostness"
that now calls you "my dear friend."
The gift of friendship that allows me to carry everything to God in prayer
is the one that has been the mainstay of my life.

A Journal Entry

Work Is a Part of the Journey

Work cannot be a byway; work is a central part of life.
All along my pilgrim pathway, I have known about work:
    I watched my parents, men and women, engaged in work.
    I sensed as a child and through the growing years
        that work will use abilities, energy, hours of time,
        much of creativity and use of many faculties,
        that work will define, in its own way,
            who we are to ourselves, to coworkers,
            to people everywhere.
In the growing up years, I wondered what work I would do in life—
    teenage years gave me part-time jobs that demanded my toil,
        that taught lessons of responsibility,
        that required me to make choices about my use of time,
        that led me on a path to work for my life journey.
In the growing-up years and into young adulthood I learned
    that work, jobs, and career are not the same;
    that work is a central life necessity—
    that I can earn my daily bread in unsatisfying work,
    that I can be an important cog in making life simpler,
    that all work is a God-given opportunity to be the best.
Finding a career that challenges, gives satisfaction,
    that may be a pathway to service for others,
    may demand special education, unique training,
    and even years of being just one of the crowd,
    may be a time of moving from job to job,
    may test endurance and willingness to just be.
A career may be just what I do, day in and day out,
    monotonous or having the potential for
    exploding into some of the finest hours of a lifetime;
        it is not just a career, but the work

that allows me to share what is

a vital and life-giving part of my journey.

Work cannot be a byway in the ways I spend my days, my years and hours;

work is a central part of life.

Work comes from the hand of God.

A Journal Entry

Play Is a Part of the Journey

Play is a single-person activity, or it can take you outside of yourself.
Showing love to an infant, in play, can be a way of learning
        about yourself, even about others,
        about connections,
        about enjoyable moments of fun,
        about how play makes you feel inside.
Play can be done by yourself in any number of games,
        play is the most fun when it is shared activity—
                either in watching sports or theater,
                or when entering into games or contests.
My connection, through play, with others in the wider world
        can cause change within myself, within my relationships,
        within my understanding of how to be with others.
Play is a word with so many ways to be used—
        can talk about a specific act in a game,
        can be another word for theater—going to see a play,
        can be about sidewalk, neighborhood games,
        can be the Olympics, something for all people worldwide,
        can be all manner of sports and recreation,
        can even be important in word usage—a play on words.
Play is an essential part of a lifetime journey:
        learning to find joy in little moments,
        moving from the ordinariness into laughter,
        exercising your body into suppleness,
        finding a necessary wholeness as I engage myself.
Playing gives me a unique and different way
        to be all that sharing myself with others is of God.

Thoughts for Reflection

Journey into the Spiritual

While all of these thoughts have been enhanced because of relationships with others, there is the sense that it still happens very close to home and in personal collaboration with those near and dear persons in close proximity. Going into areas that may mean travel, going into different cultural patterns, and expanding the circle of self into vast worlds of difference, of size, of seeing unexplored vistas of nature calls us to recognize that God has the whole world in God's hands.

There is, however, an even greater need for soul searching, for demanding that the self, in its inmost soul, continues to move into deeper relationship with the "ground of being." That way is the way of prayer that is expressed in solitary moments or in union with others.

Prayer can be simple, needing only thought transference between the deity and the self; prayer may have ritual attached or may have certain positions of the body. It may require focus and the totality of being. Prayer varies because of your understanding of who God is.

There are many different world religions, and many of these are subdivided. Each one has its own guideposts—the Bible, the Koran, the Jewish Testament, and many others. Each one has its ceremonies, its own unique rituals, a founder who is its leader, and sacred acts of commitment.

Prayer as you journey is a basic need—to be tethered to the power of the universe in such a simple way leads to a deep, profound belief in the God of all. A prayerful life demands that all of life should be lived within the love of God, in quiet moments and in humdrum occasions, in anxiety and in joyous celebrations of the power of the living God.

A Journal Entry

Praying Is a Part of the Journey

Prayer is like concentric circles—they move in their own orbit
       but blend into one another, enhance each other,
       grow into intensity with God.

Prayer Is about Form

I learned to pray at my mother's knee when I was very young—
       holding my hands clasped between my mother's hands
       in prayer position, as it was shown to me.
I learned that there were other ways to pray, even in my close circle:
       I did not have to do it in silence with closed eyes,
       I did not have to wear special clothes,
       I just needed to tap into God's presence wherever I was,
       no matter what I was doing or what was happening around me,
          conversing with God could change a situation and
          bring healing
             if I took the time to listen for God's words to me.
I learned that all around the earth there were different ways to pray—
       singing, dancing, prostrating oneself, shouting, and in groups,
       that God entered into whatever form of communication
          used by God's creation that allowed companionship
          with humans.
I learned that different religious beliefs—either my own Christianity or
       Islam, Judaism, Buddhism, Animism, or any other group
          that claims a relationship with some Being greater
          than itself
          has developed a form of prayer communication with
          that God.
Prayer is not just singular; it can be found everywhere—in occasions
of great need,

there are books of prayers, from every faith,
there are profound prayers found in the Psalms,
there are assembly prayers, coming from churches,
    from important civic occasions,
    from catastrophes and intense human need,
prayer is in the very air.

Prayer Is about Presence

As I grew older, I learned that prayer was more than just form,
Prayer was sharing my thanks, my questions, my fervent wishes
    with a Being I could not see,
    one who could help me, in some strange way, to be a good person,
    one who loved me in ways outside my understanding.
Prayer was, in my beginning years, the time of becoming acquainted
    with God's presence in my senses, my words,
        my emotions, my feelings, my family.
The midpoint was my growing intimation that there was something
more,
    that my relationship with the Creator could envelop a whole life,
    could enrich my journey into self and find a home with God.
Prayer is in the breath, the sigh, the heart,
    in the moments of exaltation because
        the Presence is felt within the sense of wholeness;
    in the moments of sadness and great need
        because that connection with Presence seems to be
        lacking.
Prayer is in the silent wanderings of the soul—
    a time of offering up my joys, my failures, myself,
    a time of pondering in God's presence all that I am,
    a time for holiness to fill my being.
Prayer and the sense of Presence is tangible and intangible,
    it is my contact with the living God,
    it will enable all my days.

Thoughts for Reflection

Journey to a Larger World

Learning that there is so much more beyond our enclosed space tells of cities, states, country, and an entire world. Such information continues to enlarge the growing vision as we move from infant to toddler to preschooler to school-age child to adolescent to young adult to middle-aged adult to older adult. Now at the midpoint, we have already absorbed the facts that will move us to try to make these facts personal; to learn what we can do to be a part of the larger whole.

It is important that we move from the individual and close family and friends into determining how outside, global events will shape the personal journey, even as it shows ramifications for the global village. We can look at events as they have affected people in the past, on a global scale, and learn from them whatever we can about ways of coping with change. Such information, leading from the personal, expands into new horizons and commits to being a factor in the global village, perhaps even to a planetary consideration.

Adulthood takes us from the past and leads us to the present, as it is known, and challenges the future in a world that constantly seeks pathways toward the unknown. The journey never stops, the pathways are ever enlarging, and we seek guidance in acknowledging that one person lives in a vast universe.

A Journal Entry

Neighborhood

During the passing of the years, I have been aware
that my sense of self cannot be a solitary event,
      that I have been influenced by what is happening
           in my neighborhood, in my city,
           in my state and other states as well,
           in my country, in the wide world.
What is a neighborhood? What makes up its parts?
      Neighborhoods are often unique to one person,
      neighborhoods can mean the same to many people,
      neighborhoods can change
           if we move from one place to another,
           if it is related to a specific culture,
           if it is part of ethnicity, a church or religion,
Neighborhood calls on me to fit myself into the group
      by sharing my inner self with others,
      by working for the causes and concerns of the chosen group,
      by giving and receiving what is important for the welfare
           of a specific section of geography,

Cities

But what of the areas beyond the closeted section of a neighborhood,
when we need to reach out to encompass many circles of interest;
when it needs to be larger, more comprehensive?
     We call it a city; we name it to identify it,
          we give it specific characteristics,
          we give it boundaries, literal and figurative,
          we claim its good points—the way it helps us,
          we try to dismiss what is not pretty or laudable.
In my middle years when I understand myself in adult ways,
       do I have a responsibility to make my city something more?
       Do I work out my concern for the homeless, the hungry?
       How do I see change in myself as a means to change a city?
A city is so big, so varied, has so many demands, calls out for help
       to a whole populace, to numerous other people;
       why do I believe that it should be my mission?
       Why do I sense a call to be a spokesperson for my city?

State

Moving on to yet another geographic sense, I look at the word *state*.
I look back to my journey into words and recognize that this word
      needs to be journaled into varied usage and creates its own
      journey,
      both as a part of the outer and inner world.
I am a member of a state, perhaps have been in several states;
      each has its own name, its own geographic boundaries:
I am a citizen of my state; I expect to be given
      rules to live by, protection from many kinds of problems,
      an education, a means to earn a living,
      a government that gives equal rights to all,
      allows me to be a productive personage within the larger context.
I have moved even further from that knowledge of self as one individual:
      into a person who keeps creating wider and wider circles of
      concern,
      into becoming someone who looks for larger dreams,
      into a committed citizen who will share the journey with others.
My pathway into the word *state* leads into a different direction;
      state can tell us of a mode of being—medical issues,
      of a current status, of various conditions that explain
            emotions, feelings, and just plain everydayness.
Any given day I could say: I am in a state of confusion, or
      this state is bewildering, or the day holds me in a state of
      happiness.
I wonder how many states I could pass through in a lifetime.
If I am blessed I rejoice that the best state
      permits me to make of each day a time of wonder.
Speaking out in metered ways the very truths that I have learned
      from the beginning up until the midpoint is reassuring—
      enough so that I feel confident to share with others
      the "state" of my life, these words that are uniquely me.
The God of love walks with me on this stated journey.

Country

I claim the United States as my country, the place of my birth and
citizenship,
There are so many of us, and each citizen holds dear
   the many facets that make up our country.
There are many countries and each is special
     to those who offer allegiance to the land and
     seek to be enveloped with everything that is worthy
     of trust.
Country is so wide-ranging – it allows each boundaried land to be
   a home, a part of a larger family,
   to be filled with valleys, hills, oceans, and lakes,
   firm footage for innumerable miles of beauty and wonder,
   to be God's footprint in my native land.
Country can be so circumscribed: vast outreaches of farmland
   small rural villages that lie outside large cities,
   open countryside that harbors little habitation
     and brings little of worth in dry space of the planet.
Country is diversity, sharing itself with all humankind.
   It compels me to reach out to those who have little,
   to those who are hungry, homeless, care-ridden,
   who yearn to feel that someone, perhaps me,
     will move beyond the self, into wider spheres,
     and want to walk in tandem with others' needs.

World

This byway that I take into the world causes me to go
  back to the self and increase the complexity
  of the influences that have shown me a new way.
I have been by myself, then added family, neighborhood,
  city, state, country, and I have come to the world.
World, as a word, is a behemoth, too big to understand in its fullness,
  too varied, and yet, it has smallness.
  it encompasses many truths in its great variety.
There is the world of space, the world of fun,
  the world of knowledge, the animal world,
  the scientific world—how many other worlds, I can only guess.
From all these worlds, I know that they make up *the world*,
  but so much more awesome, so almost ungraspable.
I am one person, one tiny being in a vast planet,
  seeking to be myself and knowing that
  these varied worlds, this world of unlimited knowledge
    has the power to change me,
     to cause new dimensions in my life and many other lives
     and in the interconnectedness to show forth God's glory.
  I am a small figure in a large world;
    what I do, say, feel has consequences far beyond myself.
    Who I am in God's plan will change me, change others,
     make a world within the worlds God has made.

The Ending of the Journey

Thoughts for Reflection

The Journal of the Journey's End

All along the lifetime journey we are bombarded by growth and diminishment, by sameness and change, and by following known and unknown paths. As the years pass, we learn to cope with all the vagaries of existence. Time, that in younger years seemed to move with miniscule passing, has now become the speedy movement of the years. Where once we could learn to adjust to what happens in both the personal world and the world at large, now it requires more diligence to fit into a world in which there is less time available for living.

While we never know at what moment the ending will come, we see some certainties that come in the latter years of life. Almost assuredly, along the way will come some form or forms of illness that teach us how to live in spite of pain. Aging changes everyone, physically, mentally, and spiritually. And yet there is acceptance of who we are in these later years.

So much that makes up the journey has woven in and out of our place on earth that we may find a unique pattern that leads to an ending. There is a settledness that can accept the unknown and find, in remembering, the blessings that have been the journey; that will find anticipation in the little moments of movement on the ending journey; that may allow the giving of love to all we meet.

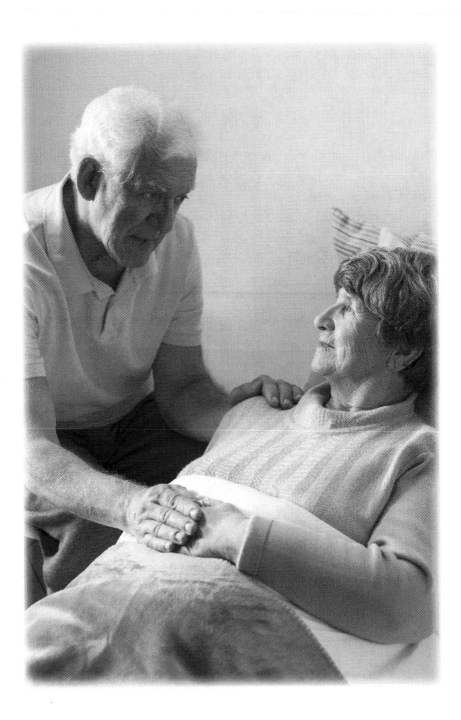

A Journal Entry

Aging—the Mainline of the Journey

This journey to aging began without my knowledge,
> tattooed itself into my very being.

A journey demands traveling, moving from place to place,
> traveling through days and years and decades of my life,
> traveling on different highways and byways,
> traveling according to a plan or unexplained ways,
> trusting that God who knows my human plan will lead me
>> to my aged ending point.

Living my life has one constant—day by day, I grow older;
> it happens without my even thinking about it,
> it changes me in miniscule ways, but it is a fact of life.

Aging happens all along my journey, from beginning point to ending point.

As I come to the ending point, there are signs of aging that show themselves—
> my body changes from freewheeling movement,
> my body thickens, becomes more flaccid, loses tone,
> wrinkles begin to show themselves,
> aches and pains are more frequent.
> I cannot move as quickly, I cannot do as many activities as I did before,
> memory may go, my thoughts processes are slower—I am slower.

I know I am an elder, an old lady in terms of years,
> inside me I still see all that makes me "me,"
> but others assure me that I do not seem my age,
>> that I don't seem old, still have great energy.
> I say, "This is me, old in years, and this is who I am.
>> I cherish this being who has lived these years,

and now sings praises to the God who walked with me
into my elderhood."
The early tattoos have lost their color, have stretched to cover a wider
body,
now merely serve as reminders of what once was,
now indicate that life has moved along,
and yet the tattoos will be there until the end—
still along the highway of God's plan.

A Journal Entry

Illness Is a Byway on the Journey

Illness is common to everyone in some form—
> it is a part of all life from beginning point and midpoint
> and seems to be heaviest in those years leading to the end point.

As I approach the ending years of life, I ponder why
> some people seem to go through much of life unscathed,
> some seem to have much more than their share
> > of petty illness, minor aches and pains;
> some run the gamut of the really major diseases,
> > such as cancer, heart problems,
> > accidents that require surgery,
> > mental and even spiritual problems,
> > and an unending list of serious complaints.

This byway, this matter of illness, causes disruption in my journey—
Minor illnesses allow me to continue my regular living style,
> with discomfort, loss of time to do my work well,
> and need for drugs to hasten healing.

Major causes of disruption cause me to find a new pathway on my journey—
> loss of body parts requires learning different skills,
> and may lead to a new vocation or avocation—
> > the developing of a different lifestyle that will alter my living.
> loss of mental acuity from any number of causes
> may make of me a person who has lost the unique self that always has been,
> > who has left the former pathway and needs a change in journey.
> loss of former abilities because of the serious, ultimately death-dealing illnesses,

means becoming comfortable with guiding myself
through
much of pain, through needing help from others,
becoming patient, seeking joys in other ways,
in giving and accepting help and love from friends,
in knowing that my inner beauty is still deep inside me.
Illness has caused whatever has happened to me on my journey
to recognize that this byway, these many facets of the trip,
have now become my major highway,
my journey has turned from the straight, planned way
to a pathway in which God leads this journeyer
to an earthly ending.

Thoughts for Reflection

The Journey in Panoply

In these later years leading to an ending, we find that the journey has slowed, that there is a difference in desires and needs; we do not plan ahead in the same way; we treasure the little moments, the personal relationships, the adventure that lies ahead, still clothed in mystery.

We have the realization of how far we have come on the journey through the years of growth, knowledge, and understanding; through just being within the self and knowing how that self has changed; through how that self has walked the highways and byways of the journey and now moves with slow tread into the ending.

In these years, remembrance and contemplation may define the persona of the journeyer, may help to show a meaningful way to an ending, and may even acknowledge the plan of God for our lifetime journey.

Remembrance allows us to walk again through past events and memories. There is also a part of the definition that a remembrance, a token, may be a gift. Often people do something tangible by giving a gift to help them remember some special occasion.

Remembrance may be a part of contemplation—the recognition of what has led us to be contemplative, mindful of ourselves and where the journey will lead; mindful of the interconnection with family, world, and God.

Contemplation keeps us in the present moment, focusing on specific thoughts or plans, and seeking a pathway toward the future that now is more limited by fewer years in which to find the self that will be in God's plan, as the days and years come to an ending.

The latter years open up more time, more desire to think through what we have accomplished, what we yet feel must be done to be in harmony with God's will. So much of life from its beginning through the midpoint has been spent in activity, work, service, and helping others so that now it seems a necessity to go deeper, deeper into where the Spirit leads. Fellowship, in closer companionship with the Holy One, may demand understanding the contemplative life.

There are many guideposts to facilitate the journey, byways that may still bring us to the highway of entry into the rooms of God's heavenly home.

A Journal Entry

Remembrance—Steps to a Journey's Ending

At the ending point it is not strange to find myself
      making return trips to other byways, other events,
      but doing this while remaining in one place.
How would I do this journey in remembrance?

There was a picture that I recalled that beckoned to me—
      it was quite stark, having only a rosary necklace as the main
      focus.
      The beads looped up and around simple stick drawings of
      events and people,
      until it ended at the bottom of the page,
            tying together the important part of a person's life,
            indicating that all of life was entwined in God and
            prayer.
Here was the vehicle that I would use as I stepped back in memory.
      as I remembered the old times of the journey,
      I would find some beads to act as my rosary;
      as I caressed each bead, I would offer up a prayer
            in joyous thanksgiving for the wonder of memory
            and the roadways that changed the journey,
                that led to this moment.

Pictures

It made sense that my first bead of remembrance should come
in looking at pictures of so many kinds;
photographs, postcards, old movies,
computer images, CDs, those pictures hung upon walls,
paintings done by family, friends, and by great
artists.
As I hold the bead that represented pictures, I felt enclosed
in warmth that spanned the ages, in timely love, and in just
feeling,
so that when I lift up each picture, I hold the bead
and praise the Lord of all for these treasures.

Souvenirs

Souvenir collecting runs rampant through our civilization—it is done everywhere.
Traveling around the world permits finding treasures in expected places,
    but finding the rare, the unusual, the one-of-a-kind artifacts
    brings unexpected joy and lifts my spirits in total gladness.
The souvenirs, collected from a small child's artwork,
    those drawings that are found on refrigerator doors,
    the little special gifts that hold a sacred place within my home,
    the souvenirs that are stamped on my heart,
        tattooed, never to be forgotten.
I hold tightly the rosary bead that lifts these memories
    to great heights of thoughtfulness and loving care,
        and praise the Lord of all for these treasures.

Events

I look back on holidays and walk in happy steps to parade watching—
>as I think of national remembrance days of great leaders,
>of days of no school and the freedom
>>to just play, go willy-nilly on my own,
>fun times: trick-or-treating, and the goodies delivered,
>awesome Thanksgiving feasts that include extended family,
>Christian holidays: Easter, Christmas, Lenten season,
>>times to feed my soul, to be in God's presence.
I know that there are other events that are more personal:
>getting a driver's license, my first voting thrill,
>completing my schooling, my first job,
>marriage, family born into my home, loss of family,
I think I could use more than one bead to share memories,
>holding many beads, caressing each one as I remember,
>visualizing what effect each one had on my life,
>knowing that undergirding all such events
>>can become holy days within my memory,
>>and then I will praise the Lord of all for these treasures.

People/Special Persons

Over the years, from beginning to ending, there have been people
that I cannot forget, that I want to include in my lifetime memories,
There are the easy, most important ones that cover all the years:
     parents, siblings, related family persons,
     my school teachers who taught me lessons for living,
     friends who shared delight and sadness—
     these I count on in my daily living.
I know that there have been select persons who have come to me
     through books, lectures, even by means of television and
     computer.
I cannot offer enough gratitude to those friends who stood by my side
     when life was difficult, when I needed a warm clasp, a hug,
     when I wanted advice, when I needed someone to just be.
All the other memories require people, special persons
     to make important the pictures, souvenirs, and events,
     but it is the loyal, lovely, caring people that shout out
          the love that touches the heart.
Here I sit, holding almost all the rest of the rosary beads, crumpled
together,
     as my special people are crumpled together within my heart.
I believe I can use more of these beads to solidify memories—
     holding so many beads, takes more time to caress each one
     in remembrance
     visualizing what effect each one had on my life,
     knowing that undergirding all such remembrances, they will
          become holy days within my being,
     and then I will praise the Lord of all for these treasures.

God

Looped through all these rosary beads, looped through all of my remembrances
> is trust in the love of God, unending and ever faithful.
> There is remembrance that God has called me by name and
> > that I must be true to that calling,
> > living into that name from a God of love.
As I look at all the places that I have prayed for in this rosary,
> as I hold the beads, I offer my prayer of thanksgiving, knowing
> > that undergirding all such remembrances,
> > God offers unending love.
God's remembrance gift permits my life to become an alleluia.
> I will offer my praise to the Lord of all being
> > for God's presence within me
> > and for all these treasures found in my rosary beads.

A Journal Entry

Contemplative Living—Steps toward a Journey's Ending

Contemplation is a word that has many meanings, related to thinking:
  reflection, thoughtfulness, introspection,
  observing, rumination, studying, and numerous other ways
  to define it.
Contemplation is more than just a word; it involves the deepening of
one's spirit:
  in Eastern religions, it is seen as a form of yoga,
  in Christian spirituality, it is prayer and meditation,
  and in ordinary practice it reflects much time in deep thought.
There are universal principles among all religions:
  the need for the whole body, mind and emotions to be involved
  using focus points; literature, the arts, thought, and prayer
      in order to develop awareness and insight
          to the connection to the divine.
In these years, stretched from midpoint toward the penultimate,
  I have discovered that more time is available to me,
  I have gone back into my history, remembered the good, the
  sad, the beautiful.
  I have counted my blessings for all that has gone before—the
  past and the present.
In these years, stretched from midpoint toward the penultimate,
  I am impressed with the need to find myself more in tune
  with the Infinite.
  I want to walk the byway of contemplation, seeking
  transformation.
  I want to spend hours, days and months in touch with the
  God of all.
      this for me says contemplation.
What does it mean to be contemplative? How shall I begin?

I begin by going apart, by searching for a committed time
or times,
I begin to understand the need to have an open mind,
the meaning of centering, to be deeply attentive to myself,
> becoming aware of all the ways in which I can achieve
> calm.
The use of the many rituals that may lead into the sense of
the holy---
> centering prayer, that may need constant repeating,
> the *lectio divina* that sheds light through scripture,
> sacred words that show many paths to spiritual discipline,
> walking the labyrinth, and sharing in vigils
>> so that the motion of the body will call out
>> the sacred,
> the need to listen for the still voice that blots out all
> other sound.
Learning for myself the paths that allow me to be contemplative,
> daring to offer myself in all ways into God's will,
> as I make a byway become a main highway
>> for the journey into whatever the future holds
>> for the ending into eternity!
May my contemplative journey through whatever time is mine,
> through whatever means I use to make my spiritual journey
> complete,
>> be creative, relational, generative, experiential,
>> radical, practical, generative and transformative,
>> and may I use what I learn in the deep stillness
>>> to find where my pathway will lead in the days
>>> ahead
>>> and how to act as a witness to God's great love.

Thoughts for Reflection

The Journey into Self—the Later Years

It seems only right to come back to the journey into self. It is a beginning and ending of this journal of a lifetime. The person who makes up the story is not the same in any respect—bodily, mentally, emotionally, spiritually. The years have taken their toll.

The body requires many aids to the various senses. Being older means that we cannot walk as well, if at all. We are more prone to many illnesses that sap the strength and even the will to keep on the pace of earlier living. Life tends to be more circumscribed in these later years. The sense of self may outweigh the bodily impairments and present a strong path to make the later years fully developed.

Mentally, we become forgetful, spend more time in backward looking and acknowledging the present than in developing long-range plans. However, in doing creative work, there is the same desire to be an even better worker, so that we can carry a part of ourselves as a final tribute to a life well lived.

Emotions are always a mixed-up part of our lives, difficult to accept, difficult to control, and subject to so many outside factors. We have had to be aware of how they affect our bodies, our entire selves. Changing how we live day by day and react to others is always a part of what we show to the world. In the later years we may have learned control, acceptance, and the need for support from others. Or we may have lost control and become difficult, unable to really share life with others.

As we have journeyed through the years, we may have forgotten that God is still there and wandered away, and so the deeply spiritual side has been lost. In that sense, these years may not note any change.

Serenity and acceptance and deep trust in a God of love may be the response of years of spiritual discipline. Moving from childlike faith in God to understanding innately that we are still beloved children and should be a reflection of that creative God alters our very beings.

Thoughts for Reflection

Cloud of Unknowing

After all the remembrance and contemplation, we come to the place of the unknown—what may only be conjecture. There cannot be an answer in this life about the reality of what happens in the last moments—in the passing over into God's eternity. We may have trust and believe that the loving God will be a part of the final ending journey. We may be uncertain. Thoughts about the ending can be encapsulated, but there will be no journal written about the journey to God's creative movement in this life and whatever comes in the beyond.

This is ephemeral, like clouds. We can look at the sky on a beautiful, clear day and notice that there are white fleecy clouds that hide a portion of the sky, but light may be reflected through it. Reflected through this final journey, we will find an understanding of how the cloud speaks to the yet unknown of how God will speak to the children of the promise.

Four words relate to clouds that help us understand this phenomenon of that moment in time and space:

- a cloudy day, with its promise of rain and change in conditions
- clouds themselves with their infinite variety
- the Cloud, in computer language
- *The Cloud of Unknowing,* a fourteenth-century book on contemplation and the pathway to a close relationship with God

Many other similes and metaphors could be used to conclude this book and its journal entries and its "Thoughts for Reflection." Keeping it simple by using only one is, in itself, a journey to come, at last, to the unknown.

A Journal Entry

Journeying Days

My journal began with the words:
"The journey began without my knowledge,
It began in a dream between two people—
That early dream tattooed itself into my very being."
Today, many, many years later, it is my dream,
      tattooed into a body that has known much of living.

All of the journal entries tell the story
      of how this pilgrim, this journeyer,
        wandered, planned, set goals, lived day by day,
        and created my unique life that leads into journey's end.
These years, this lifetime has been filled with such a wealth of
awareness—
      family that has developed and enlarged,
      friends and some enemies,
      teachers, guides, leaders, and just ordinary people,
      the gurus who caused me to think new thoughts,
      children who brought joy and stress,
      the needy ones who called on me to give of myself.
Now there are many tattoos not found on my body
      but drawn on my soul, found deep within me,
      that will determine these later years.
Increasingly, as my journal entries indicate,
      I lift my tattooed soul to the God
      who created the journey that is me.
I open these words that summarize what my journey has been
      and the faith that has led me through the journey.
God has walked with me and blessed me beyond imagining,
      has loved me through the everydayness of life,
      has shown the way through all the years.

God holds out a hand to guide me into the uncertain time
      that leads beyond my earthly journey
      into mystical union with the Ground of Being.
I grasp the hand of God and trust that all my length of days,
      of hours and months, of stretched-out years
            will carry me to the safe harbor of God's eternal love.

A Journal Entry

A Cloudy Day

It is a cloudy day, and my thoughts about an ending
      swirl around like so many clouds,
      changing colors, stomping on top of one another,
      hinting of the possibility of change,
      or just staying in monotone grayness,
      being impossible to know for what to plan,
         or just to allow the cloudiness to wash over me.
In these later years there is a clouded vision of
      my place in this world of unparalleled change,
      what all the years of being me portends for the future,
      what hopes there may be that the sun
         will break through and give me some guidance
         as I go step by step into the unknown days ahead.
Beyond the clouds, beyond the turmoil of a changing sky,
      beyond the threatening disasters of the coming years,
      beyond even the joyous hours of life under a gray sky,
      beyond the ordinary that all may experience,
         I know that God is there within all of the unknown.
I walk into the cloudy days of the unknown future,
      trusting that in God's plan for me, I will be safe,
      trusting that as I come to the ending days, God will
         lift the grayness and that there will be no fear,
trusting that in the sunshine of God's love
         that I can touch the hand of God and dwell
         with the one who created my journey.

A Journal Entry

Clouds

There are so many things I can say about clouds;
> so many shapes, so many sizes,
> so much fun to look at and guess what I can see within the
> cloud,
> so fleecy and also so grim,
> similar to earth with little valleys, piled on places that speak
> of hills,
> they can be small or massive or completely covering the sky.
Clouds have a variety of colors, clouds can be reflectors—
> watching a sunrise or sunset,
> seeing the transforming beauty of the times of day,
>> I know that sun and clouds
>> make the sky a veritable palette of majestic color.
Sun breaking through the clouds heralds a change in weather,
> and allows the clouds to be harbingers of good cheer.
Rain, pouring much needed water to a thirsty earth,
> may also create a time of rejoicing.
All the variety and contours of the clouds, their necessity in our sky,
> speak daily of the Creator's plan to care for
>> the children of earth in abundant measures;
> teach us lessons of humility and joyous thankfulness.
The variety, contours and changeableness of the clouds
> add to the lessons I may learn in hours of converse with the
> clouds:
> that on my journey I may not fear the clouds,
> that on my journey, the clouds will speak of God's wisdom,
> that the journey will move across vast spaces
>> and lead my ending to my God.

A Journal Entry

The Computer Cloud

The clouds in the sky are natural, part of what I live with daily.
The computer Cloud, however, is a human invention,
      relatively new in terms of centuries, even of thought—
The computer Cloud uses a network of remote servers
       to store, manage, and process data that has been placed on
       the Internet, rather than with a local server.
Data in the Cloud requires security and privacy and must
      include how to store and make further use of the material,
      understanding the vast glossary of terms related to the Cloud:
          most are ordinary terms used in everyday living but
          having a whole new context as they relate to this Cloud.
Trying to find the relationship of this Cloud to my life has led
      to wondering what is so important in my life that
      I have filed it in some other place so that I can retrieve it.
My remote storage places exist in so many locations:
      a filing cabinet, an attic cubby hole,
      on my computer Cloud (I am a person who could do this),
      in a secret place that only I can know,
      in my memory trove and special remembrances,
      tattooed on my very soul.
Managing, retrieving, and processing these Cloud items for use
      in my later years;
      for adding to my sense of self as I walk into the ending years,
      means I must make decisions about the value of all items in
      the Cloud.
      Are there some that will enhance the years left?
      Are there some that can be dumped because they have served
      their purpose?
      Are there those that will be a part of my estate?
      Are there those tattooed on my soul that will remain forever?

I wonder how my decisions will be reflected in God's plan for my
life—

> how will I manage the journey, both within the facts
> > that have been stored and the daily living of these
> > years?
In all of the clouds, as shown in this journal, may I seek God's will
> and trust the ending to the Creator God

A Journal Entry

The Cloud of Unknowing

There is yet another cloud that comes to me.
It is from a fourteenth-century book called *The Cloud of Unknowing*.
It is the most contemplative source of my clouds
        and seems appropriate to make another deeply spiritual entry
        in my journal.
I do not need to restate my thoughts on contemplation
        because all that I considered from before in my life still holds
        true,
        and all those reflections have been my connection to the Infinite.
As I read in *The Cloud* and learn from absorbing the mystics' faith,
        I need to lift up in new contemplation
            some words that lead into nearness to God.

Mind—learning to focus my mind and thought is a demand from
the cloud,
        sharpening my mind to look outside the strictures of the box,
        finding the roadway to come to God
            fully engaged with thinking through God's mind.

Imagination—clouds offer many opportunities to see in new dimensions,
        where God would lead a mind attuned to fantasy and vision.
        How do I envision the wonders of a world that could be more?
        How could I imagine a world filled with God's love?

Reason—after imagination has taken flight and the mind has focused,
        after the pondering, I seek the way for reason
            to lead me into daring new reasons for making my
            choices,
            to lead me to make the choices of what is good, what
            is of God.

From all kinds of clouds and especially of the Unknowing Cloud,
> I need my own will to move me toward the choices of God,
>> to what is good, to knowing that my self is now fully open
>>> to the highway that will stretch to God's eternity.

May I see in the darkness shattered by God's light, in the opening of the clouds—-

> the byway to the unknown as I trust all to God in prayer,
> a new relationship to the pathway of my life's ending,
> to understand that the Divine has inundated me with grace,
> and that God is my life in the spirit and that God's road leads to endless day,
> to rediscover that the clouds have led me from the unknown
>> into the assurance of the known love of God's eternal kingdom.

Epilogue

The last pages of the journal written by Lydia have completed the *Journaling of the Byways of Lifetime Journeys*. We see a life crisscrossed with roadways, intersections, byways, and learning experiences. It was a unique life but not an unusual movement through the years. These were the words (placed in a journal), plus the thoughts and actions of a person committed to journey into a life that has an ending in human form. Life in God's eternal kingdom is the next part of the journey.

In a book of poetry I wrote many years ago, I concluded with a poem, which I quote, with some adaptations in select verses. These words seem a fitting ending to this book.

Audrey Brown Lightbody

Eternity in My Hand[7]

Eternity is little bits and pieces
      fashioned into an ending
      little bits and pieces
          of myself, my world, the universe,
          of the empowering God.
I hold the little bits and pieces,
      I hold eternity in my hand.
I see myself as I have been, as I am now,
      but know that there is yet
      a part of me that will lead me into
          new pathways, new commitments.
I hold within my grasp the little bits and pieces
      of myself that will become the me of all eternity.
I know that God is there within and part
      of all the mysteries that will unfold
          as I seek the avenue to eternity.
There is a God I cannot see who holds
      within that empowering hand
          all the bits and pieces that I scarcely can fathom.
I know with certainty that all my life—
      however long that may be—
      when looked at in the light of eternity
          is hidden fast with the God,
             who looked at all creation,
             and claimed it "good."
Whatever the future holds, it will be
      empowered by the God who holds me
      in that hand through all eternity.
I hold eternity in my hand, fashioned into an ending,
      fashioned into God's beginning!

Amen   Alleluia   Amen

Notes

1. Journey (n.d.) *Merriam-Webster Dictionary*. Retrieved May 22, 2017 from http//merriam-webster.com/dictionary/journey.
2. Quote is from my book *Faith is the Journey,* published by R. C. Law & Co. Inc. in 1987.
3. I have quoted from words in my previous book *Ordinary Fragments,* published by West Bow Press in 2012, and adapted some of the words to fit this story.
4. Ibid.
5. Music (n.d.). John Denver. Retrieved May 22, 2017, from http//www.goodreads.com/quote 283847-music.
6. Emotions (n.d.). *Dictionary.com Unabridged.* Retrieved May 22, 2017 from http://www.dictionary.com/browse/emotions/
7. The quote for this poem is taken from my book *Fragmented Senses,* published by Outskirts Press in 2006.